## Holiday ★ Histories

# Halloween

Jennifer Blizin Gillis

Heinemann Library
Chicago, Illinois

© 2003 Heinemann Library
a division of Reed Elsevier Inc.
Chicago, Illinois

Customer Service   888–454–2279
Visit our website at www.heinemannlibrary.com

Page layout by Ginkgo Creative, Inc.
Printed and bound in the United States by Lake Book Manufacturing, Inc.

07 06 05
10 9 8 7 6 5 4 3 2

**Library of Congress Cataloging-in-Publication Data**
Gillis, Jennifer Blizin, 1950-
   Halloween / Jennifer Blizin Gillis.
      p. cm. — (Holiday histories)
Summary: Presents background information on the origins and traditions
of customs related to the celebration of Halloween.
   ISBN 1-4034-3506-5 (HC), 1-4034-3691-6 (Pbk.)
   1. Halloween—Juvenile literature. [1. Halloween. 2. Holidays.] I.
Title. II. Series.
   GT4965.G56 2003
   394.2646—dc21
                                    2003007826

**Acknowledgments**
The author and publishers are grateful to the following for permission to reproduce copyright material:

Cover photograph by Ariel Skelley/Corbis

p. 4 Charles Gupton/Corbis; pp. 5, 16, 23 Bettmann/Corbis; p. 7 Elizabeth Watt Photography/Stock Food; pp. 8, 20 Mary Evans Picture Library; pp. 9, 12, 21, 26, 28 Hulton Archive/Getty Images; p. 10 Bob Winsett/Index Stock Imagery, Inc.; p. 11 Stapleton Collection/Corbis; p. 13 Roger Wood/Corbis; p. 14 Erich Lessing/Art Resource, NY; p. 15 Historical Picture Archive/Corbis; pp. 17, 27 The Advertising Archive/Picture Desk; p. 18 Alinari/Art Resource, NY; p. 19 Rykoff Collection/Corbis; p. 22 Underwood & Underwood/Corbis; p. 24 Gaslight Advertising Archives Inc.; p. 25 Superstock; p. 29 Mario Tama/Getty Images

Photo research by Kathy Creech

Every effort has been made to contact copyright holders of any material reproduced in this book. Any omissions will be rectified in subsequent printings if notice is given to the publisher.

Some words are shown in bold, **like this.** You can find out what they mean by looking in the glossary.

# Contents

# It's Halloween!

Outside it is cold and dark. But the streets are full of children dressed in costumes. They run from house to house and ring the doorbells. Then they call out, "Trick or Treat!"

For many years, children have dressed up for Halloween. On October 31, they go around their neighborhoods collecting candy. But where did the idea of Halloween come from?

★

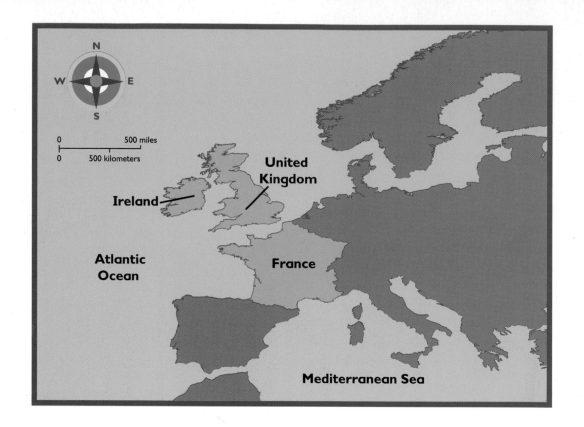

# A New Home

Halloween came from the United Kingdom. In the 1800s, thousands of **immigrants** came to the United States from parts of the United Kingdom. They brought their **customs** to their new country. In Ireland, people had celebrated Halloween for many years.

Irish children collected food and money
on October 31. Families ate colcannon,
a dish of mashed potatoes, parsnips, and
onions. Parents hid money or a ring in the
colcannon for the children to find.

★

# Celtic New Year

Halloween was a custom that started with the **Celts.** The Celts were people who lived in what are now the countries of England, Ireland, Scotland, and France. The Celts believed that the New Year began on November 1.

On October 31, they had a **festival** called
**Samhain.** Samhain was a **harvest** festival.
The Celts thanked their gods for good
**crops.** People ate fall fruits and vegetables.

# Bonfires

Some people build bonfires on Halloween for fun. But bonfires was part of **Samhain.** The **Celts** believed that when the old year ended spirits and ghosts could come back to life. So they lit big fires to keep away the ghosts.

First, people put out the fires in their fireplaces. Then, everyone went to an all-night bonfire. They burned **crops** and animals to honor their gods. In the morning, they took coals from the bonfire back to their houses to start the first fire of the new year.

# Apples

Some people bob for apples on Halloween.
Long ago, the **Romans** took over parts of
England, Scotland, Ireland, and France.
They introduced their **customs** to the **Celts.**
The Romans had an important fall holiday,
too. This holiday honored a goddess
named Pomona.

*This is a Roman mosaic of a bird sitting on an apple.*

Pomona was the goddess of apples and trees. Apples were another **crop** that people **harvested** in the fall. Soon, feasts on October 31 included apples.

# A New Holiday

Hundreds of years after the **Romans** and the **Celts,** people still had a fall holiday called "All Hallows Day." On November 1, people honored family members who had died. The night before the holiday was called "All Hallows Eve." Soon, people shortened the name to "Hallowe'en."

On Hallowe'en, poor people went from
house to house asking for food and money.
Sometimes they dressed in costumes or did
funny stunts. People gave them a few pennies
and special treats called "soul cakes."

# Witches and Black Cats

People think the word "witch" came from old English. Long ago, women in England who made medicines from plants were called "wise women." The old English word for wise woman was *wicca*.

*This old picture shows two witches making a brew.*

Some people believed that witches had power over cats. Most cats looked black in the dark. Their eyes glowed when light shone on them. So some people believed that it was bad luck to see a black cat on Halloween.

*A black cat with an arched back is a very old Halloween symbol.*

# Jack O' Lantern

In the United Kingdom, people sometimes saw lights shining over swamps and fields at night. The lights may have been from a kind of gas that comes out of swamps. But some people believed lantern men, or lost spirits, were trying to find their way home. People told scary stories about them.

Many stories were about a lantern man named Jack. Jack was full of tricks. When he died, he could not get into heaven. Instead, he wandered the earth carrying a light inside a turnip. On Halloween, people put candles inside turnips and told stories about Jack O'Lantern.

*This old Halloween card shows a lantern man about to eat a pumpkin pie.*

★

19

# Pumpkins

There were few pumpkins in England, Ireland, or Scotland. But **immigrants** from those countries brought their scary stories about Jack O'Lantern to the United States. They saw that pumpkins were a popular fall food.

*In this old picture, a Scottish boy wearing a kilt swings a Jack O'Lantern to scare a man playing the bagpipes.*

Pumpkins were easy to grow. It was easy
to carve scary faces on the empty shells.
The carved pumpkins made good lanterns.
So people began to use pumpkins to make
Halloween Jack O'Lanterns.

# Costumes

Some **Celts** wore animal masks and skins to the bonfire at **Samhain.** They thought ghosts could not recognize them if they wore costumes. Later, poor people sometimes wore masks or costumes when they asked for food and money on Hallowe'en. But costumes really became popular in the United States around 1920.

At first, costumes were homemade. Parents made costumes of storybook characters. But as movies became popular, children wanted to dress like their favorite movie character. Some movie companies began making costumes of their cartoon characters.

*In the 1950s, Mickey Mouse and Felix the Cat were popular cartoon characters. Children wore costumes that showed their favorite cartoon characters.*

# Tricks and Treats

THE SATURDAY EVENING POST

November 3, 1934

5c. the Copy

MARGARET CULKIN BANNING · DANIEL WILLARD

Long ago, parents did not go out with their children on Halloween. So children sometimes played tricks on their neighbors. Sometimes they took down gates, rattled windows, or tried scaring there neighbors with Jack-O-Lanterns.

By the 1930s, people wanted these tricks
to stop. They gave children candy so
they would not play tricks on them. This
is when children started to say, "Trick
or treat!" People who did not give them
candy could expect a mean trick.

★

# Candy

Giving treats on October 31 was an old idea from the United Kingdom. But giving candy for Halloween started in the United States. At first, people mostly gave out homemade candies, such as popcorn balls, taffy, and fudge. During **World War II,** sugar was hard to get. There was little trick or treating, because people were not supposed to show lights at night.

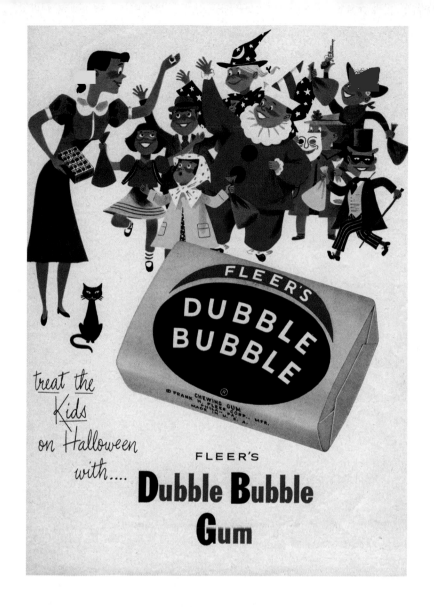

After World War II, people could eat as much sugar as they wanted. Candy makers knew that children were trick or treating at Halloween. So they advertised their candies in magazines and comic books.

# An American Holiday

Halloween started thousands of years ago in countries far away. Like many of our holidays, **immigrants** brought Halloween to the United States. Once it was a scary **custom** but now it has become a time for fun.

Today, Halloween is an American holiday.
No matter what their background,
Americans of all ages celebrate Halloween.

# Important Dates

## Halloween

| | |
|---|---|
| **500 BC** | **Celts** celebrate the fall holiday **Samhain** on October 31 |
| **100 AD** | **Romans** mix Samhain with **festival** celebrating Pomona, the goddess of the apple |
| **900 AD** | Poor people in England, Ireland, and Scotland celebrate All Hallows Eve (Hallowe'en) by going from house to house for money and food |
| **1690** | Salem witch **trial** takes place in Salem, Massachusetts |
| **1840** | Thousands of **immigrants** from Ireland come to the United States, bringing Halloween with them |
| **1900–1930** | Children begin playing tricks on their neighbors on Halloween |
| **1930** | People begin giving Halloween candy to keep children from playing tricks |
| **1940** | Sugar was hard to get during World War II |
| **1950** | Candy makers begin advertising Halloween candy and stores begin selling costumes of cartoon characters |

# Glossary

**Celts** people who lived long ago in England, Ireland, Scotland, and France.

**crop** plants grown by farmers for food and other uses

**custom** something people have done the same way for a long time

**festival** time of celebration

**harvest** to pick fruits and vegetables that have been growing

**immigrant** person who moves to a new country

**Roman** people who lived in what is now Italy from 27 BC to 312 AD

**Samhain** (You say SOW-in) Celtic New Year's Eve, celebrated each Year on October 31

**World War II** war that lasted from 1939 to 1945 in which the United States, England, France, and other countries fought Germany, Japan, and Italy

# More Books to Read

Bruchac, Joseph. *Squanto's Journey*. New York: Harcourt, 2000.

Kuperstein, Joel. *Celebrating Thanksgiving*. Mankato, Minn.: Creative Teaching Press, 1999.

Roop, Connie. *Let's Celebrate Thanksgiving*. Brookfield, Conn.: Millbrook Press, Inc., 1999.

# Index